RISE AGAIN

TRANSFORMING GRIEF INTO PURPOSE AND PASSION

WORKBOOK

WONDRA SPENCER

The workbook belongs to

_____

TABLE OF CONTENTS

HOW TO USE THE WORKBOOK: RISE AGAIN

1. Set the Intention: Before diving into the worksheets, take a moment to clarify your intentions. What are you hoping to achieve? Understanding your goals will help guide your reflections and responses.

2. Find a Quiet Space: Choose a comfortable and quiet place where you can focus without distractions. Having a calming environment will make it easier to engage deeply with the material.

3. Read the Chapters: Start by reading the chapters of the workbook carefully. Each chapter builds on the previous one, so understanding the context will enhance your reflections.

4. Complete the Worksheets: Reflective Questions: Answer the prompts in each workbook thoughtfully. Don't rush; take the time to explore your feelings and memories. Be Honest and Kind: Approach your reflections with compassion for yourself. It's important to acknowledge both challenges and strengths.

5 Workbook: Use additional space or a separate journal to expand on your thoughts. If a prompt inspires a sudden idea or memory, write it down. It is your personal workbook, so let your feelings flow.

6. Take Breaks: If you find certain topics too heavy or emotional, take a break. It's okay to step away and come back later with a fresh perspective.

7. Review Your Responses: Once you've filled out the worksheets, take time to read through your answers. It can help solidify your insights and ensure you understand the lessons and growth you've identified.

8. Reflect on Your Insights: After completing the workbook, spend some time reflecting on what you've learned about yourself and how you can apply those insights in your life moving forward.

9. Share and Connect: If you feel comfortable, share your thoughts and insights with a trusted friend or support group. Discussing your reflections can lead to further understanding and connection.

10. Revisit as Needed: The workbook is not just a one-time use tool. You can revisit it whenever you feel the need to reflect on your journey again or to check in with your growth. Using this workbook is a personal and transformative experience. Take your time and be gentle with yourself as you embark on this journey of self-discovery and healing.

Enjoy the workbook,
Wondra Spencer

INTRODUCTION

Welcome to **Rise Again:** *Transforming Grief into Purpose and Passion Workbook.* The journey is yours to embark on, an invitation to explore the depths of your experiences, both the joyous and the painful. Together, we will navigate the complex landscape of grief, loss, and the profound lessons that emerge from these challenging moments. In our lives, we all encounter heartbreak, whether through personal loss, transitions, or unforeseen challenges. While these experiences can feel overwhelming, they also provide an opportunity for growth and transformation. This workbook is designed to guide you through the process of reflecting on your past, honoring your journey, and ultimately discovering the strength and purpose that lies within you. Throughout the chapters, you will find reflective prompts and worksheets that encourage you to dig deep into your emotions, confront your challenges, and celebrate your resilience. Each section builds upon the last, leading you towards a clearer understanding of yourself and your aspirations. This introduction sets the tone for your work ahead: to embrace vulnerability, nurture self-compassion, and cultivate a renewed sense of passion for life. As you turn the pages, remember that this is not simply a workbook but a personal sanctuary—a space to reconnect with your spirit, unleash your potential, and rise again. Let's begin this transformative journey together. With each insight you gain, may you find a renewed sense of hope and purpose. Wishing you strength and healing,

Wondra Spencer

CHAPTER ONE

HEARTBREAK (PAST REFLECTION WORKSHEET)

Honoring Your Journey and Learning from Your Story

Before you build your future, take a moment to reflect on your past. The workbook invites you to explore your experiences, acknowledge your growth, and find meaning in the moments that shaped you.

1. Defining Moments

List 3–5 key experiences that have deeply impacted your life—positively or painfully.

Prompt: "What moments changed, challenged, or taught me something important?"

My defining moments:

_____

_____

_____

2. What I've Survived

Name the challenges, losses, or heartbreaks you've endured. Honor your strength.

Prompt: "What have I overcome that once felt impossible?"

I've survived:

_____

_____

_____

3. Lessons Learned

Reflect on what those experiences taught you. What wisdom did you gain?

Examples: "I learned to trust myself." "I discovered my resilience." "I found peace in letting go."

My lessons:

_____

_____

_____

4. How I've Grown

Celebrate your progress. What qualities have you developed? What habits have changed?

Prompt: "How am I different now than I was before?"

I've grown in:

_____

_____

_____

_____

5. Words I Needed Then

Write a message to your past self. What would you say to comfort, encourage, or give guidance?

Dear Past Me,

_____

_____

_____

6. What I'm Letting Go Of

Release what no longer serves you—guilt, fear, shame, or limiting beliefs.

Prompt: "What am I ready to leave behind?"

I'm letting go of:

_____

_____

_____

A Final Note

_____

_____

_____

CHAPTER TWO

FACING CHALLENGES IN COPING

Worksheet: Embracing Life's Fluctuations and Building Healthy Routines

Part 1: Reflection on Fluctuations

1. Identify Your Fluctuations

List three times in the past month when you experienced a dip in your energy or motivation.

_____

_____

_____

2. Positive Reframing

For each situation above, write a positive affirmation to remind yourself that it's okay to have ups and downs.

_____

_____

_____

Part 2: Creating a Supportive Routine

3. Daily Routine Outline: Draw or write out a structured routine that you believe will help provide stability.

Include morning, afternoon, and evening activities.

- Morning: _____

- Afternoon: _____

- Evening: _____

4. Intention Setting

At the end of each day, write one thing you achieved and one challenge you faced.

- Achievement: _____

- Challenge: _____

Part 3: Health and Well-being

5. Hydration Tracker

Track your water intake for one day. How many glasses did you drink?

- Total glasses of water: _____

6. Exercise Log Write down your physical activity for the week. Include the type of exercise and duration.

- Day 1:_____ (minutes)

- Day 2:_____ (minutes)

- Day 3:_____ (minutes)

- Day 4:_____ (minutes)

- Day 5:_____ (minutes)

- Day 6:_____ (minutes)

- Day 7:_____ (minutes)

7. Community Connection

Identify one person or group you can reach out to for support on your journey towards better health.

- Name/Group: _____

Part 4: Inspirational Notes

8. Personal Affirmation for Tough Days Write down a personal affirmation that helps you on tough days, inspired by Wondra's routine.

- _____

9. Plan for Small Acts of Self-Care

List three small acts of kindness you can do for yourself this week.

_____

_____

_____

Conclusion: Reflect on your completed worksheet. What new insights have you gained about navigating challenges in life and maintaining your health?

_____

_____

Feel free to print this out or modify any sections to fit your personal style!

CHAPTER THREE

TREASURING OUR BELOVED

Worksheet: Honoring Your Loved One Purpose

The workbook is designed to help you create a meaningful day of remembrance for your loved one. Reflect on their passions and incorporate activities that celebrate their life.

1. Special Day Selection - Choose a date: What significant date will you dedicate to honoring your loved one? (e.g., birthday, anniversary, or any meaningful date)

- _____

2. Reflection on Passions - Identify their passions: - What were some of your loved one's favorite activities, hobbies, or interests? List at least three.

- 1. _____

- 2. _____

- 3. _____

3. Activities for the Day - Plan your activities: - Based on their passions, what activities will you engage in to commemorate them? (Examples: cooking their favorite dish, spending time outdoors, listening to music they loved)

- Activity 1: _____

- Activity 2: _____

- Activity 3: _____

4. Rituals and Memory Sharing - Incorporate rituals: - What small rituals will you include on this special day? - (Examples: lighting a candle, sharing stories, creating a scrapbook)

- 1. _____

- 2. _____

5. Personal Reflections

Write a letter or share a memory: - Take a moment to jot down your thoughts or feelings in a letter to your loved one or describe a cherished memory you want to share with others on this day.

_____

_____

_____

6. Collecting Memories - Gather Items: - Consider collecting old photos, mementos, or items that remind you of your loved one to include in your celebration.

List potential items below:

- 1. _____

-2. _____

7. Shared or Personal Celebration - Decide on sharing the day: - Will you celebrate alone or invite others who knew your loved one?

- _____

8. Final Thoughts - Reflection: - How do you hope this day will impact you and those who participate?

- _____

Conclusion:

By filling out this worksheet, you are creating a meaningful plan to celebrate and honor the memory of your beloved. Remember that it's the emotional connection that truly matters.

CHAPTER FOUR

CARE FOR YOU

Self-Care and Spirituality Workbook

Section 1: Reflection on Spirituality and Well-being

1. Identify Your Spiritual Beliefs: - What are your core spiritual beliefs or values? - How do these beliefs influence your mental and emotional health?

2. Integration of Spirituality and Self-Care: - In what ways can you incorporate your spiritual beliefs into your daily self-care routine? - Write down specific activities that nourish your spirit (meditation, prayer, nature walks, etc.).

Section 2: Prioritizing Your Self-Care

3. Self-Care Practices: - List of three self-care activities you enjoy and can commit to regularly:

1._____

2. _____

3. _____

4. _____

Moments of Solitude:

- Describe a recent moment of solitude where you felt relaxed and rejuvenated.

What did you do?

How did it make you feel?

5. Overcoming Guilt:

- Reflect on a time when you felt guilty for taking time for yourself. How can you reframe that thought to acknowledge the importance of self-care?

Section 3: Seeking Support

6. Identifying Support Systems: - Who are the people in your life you can reach out to for support? List their names and how they support you (friends, family, counselors, etc.).

7. Recognizing Strength: - Write down a recent experience where you sought help or support. How did this action enhance your emotional well-being?

Section 4: Goals for Personal Growth

8. Setting Intentions: - Set one or two intentions for your journey of self-care and personal growth. What steps can you take this week to move toward these goals?

Section 5: Journal About Your Journey

9. Weekly Reflection: - At the end of each week, take a moment to reflect on your journey. Write a few sentences about your experiences with self-care, any challenges faced, and how you felt spiritually and emotionally.

Tips for Using This Workbook: - Set aside dedicated time each week to complete this worksheet. - Be honest and open with yourself, this is for your growth. - Consider sharing your reflections with someone you trust for additional support. Feel free to adjust or expand on these prompts to better fit your personal journey.

CHAPTER FIVE

PASSION & SMART GOALS

Passion & Goals Workbook

Part 1: Discover Your Passion

1. What activities ignite your enthusiasm?

- _____

- _____

2. List three things you are truly passionate about:

- _____

- _____

- _____

3. Reflect on a moment when you felt alive or inspired. What were you doing?

- _____

Part 2: Setting Goals

1. What are your short-term goals (within the next 6 months)?

- _____

- _____

2. What are your long-term goals (1 year or more)?

- _____

- _____

3. Choose one goal and transform it into a SMART goal:

- Specific: _____

- Measurable: _____

- Attainable: _____

- Relevant: _____

- Time-based: _____

Part 3: Overcoming Challenges

1. Identify a challenge you've faced recently. How did it transform you?

- _____

2. List three positive influences in your life (people, books, experiences):

- _____

- _____

- _____

3. How can these influences help you in pursuing your goals?

- _____

Part 4: Daily Motivation

1. What statement can you write to remind yourself to pursue your dreams daily?

- _____

2. How will you incorporate journaling or meditation into your routine?

- _____

3. Where will you place your goals for constant reminders?

- _____

Feel free to complete this workbook at your own pace and refer back to it as your goals and passions evolve over time.

CHAPTER SIX

DON'T STOP & KEEP GOING

Passion & Goals Workbook

Part 1: Identify Your Passion

1. What activities or topics make you feel energized and excited?

- _____

- _____

2. List three passions that you want to explore further:

- _____

- _____

- _____

3. When was the last time you felt truly fulfilled while engaging in an activity?

Describe it.

- _____

Part 2: Setting Your Goals

1. What are your short-term goals (to achieve in the next 3-6 months)?

- _____

- _____

2. What are your long-term goals (to achieve in the next 1-5 years)?

- _____

- _____

3. Choose one goal and define it using the SMART criteria:

- Specific: _____

- Measurable: _____

- Achievable: _____

- Relevant: _____

- Time-bound: _____

Part 3: Facing Challenges

1. Think of a recent challenge you encountered. How did it inspire personal growth?

- _____

2. Identify three supportive influences in your life that you can lean on during tough times:

- _____

- _____

- _____

3. What steps can you take to overcome obstacles in your path toward your goals?

- _____

Part 4: Daily Motivation

1. Write a motivational statement that you can refer to daily.

- _____

2. How will you integrate journaling or meditation into your daily routine for self-reflection?

\- _____

3. Where will you display your goals to keep them front and center in your life?

\- _____

Feel free to take your time filling out this worksheet, and revisit it regularly as you progress on your journey toward fulfilling your passions and achieving your goals!

CHAPTER SEVEN

POURING INTO YOURSELF AND UPLIFTING OTHERS

Self-Care Workbook

Reflection Prompt:

1. What does healing look like for you today?

_____

_____

_____

Self-Care Inventory:

- How many hours of sleep do I get? _____

- Do I move my body regularly? (Yes/No) _____

- Did I eat something healthy today? (Yes/No) _____

- Did I drink enough water today? (Yes/No) _____

- What brings me joy that I haven't done lately?

_____

_____

_____

- When did I last say "no" to protect my peace?

_____

_____

_____

- One Activity to Nourish Myself This Week:

_____

_____

_____

Self-Contract Example: - Full Name: _____

- Date: _____

- Goal: _____

- Consequences of not meeting my goal: _____

- Rewards for meeting my goal: _____

- Completion Date: _____

- Signature: _____

- Date: _____

Reminder: - Make sure to prioritize restful sleep, aim for at least 30 minutes of exercise five days a week, and embrace activities that recharge you. This workbook serves as a guide to ensure you are nurturing your well-being and preparing to uplift others. Feel free to fill in your responses and customize the sections to best fit your needs!

Below is a self-contract; you are welcome to revise it as needed!

Here's an example of how you can structure your self-contract:

- Full Name: [Your Full Name]

- Date: [Current Date]

- Goal: [Specific Goal Related to Weight Management or Personal Development]

- Consequences of not meeting my goal: [Consequences you set for yourself]

- Rewards/reinforcements for meeting my goal: [Rewards or treats for yourself]

- Completion Date: [Your Deadline]

- Signature and Date: [Your Signature and Date]

CHAPTER EIGHT

REJOICE AND EMBRACE!

Self-Care Worksheet

1. Self-Care Inventory

- How many hours of sleep do I get each night? _____

- Do I move my body regularly? (Yes/No) _____

- Did I eat something healthy today? (Yes/No) _____

- Did I drink enough water today? (Yes/No) _____

- What brings me joy that I haven't done lately? _____

- When did I last say "no" to protect my peace? _____

2. Weekly Self-Care Commitment

- Choose one hour each week to do something that nourishes you. What will you do? _____

3. Reflection Prompts

- What does healing look like for you today?

_____

_____

- What small act of self-kindness can you offer yourself this week?

_____

_____

4. Self-Contract

- Full Name: _____

- Date: _____

- Goal: _____

- Consequences of not meeting my goal: _____

- Rewards/reinforcements for meeting my goal: _____

- Completion Date: _____

- Signature and Date: _____

5. Additional Notes

- Use this space for any other thoughts, affirmations, or insights related to your self-care journey.

_____

_____

_____

Reminder:

You cannot pour from an empty cup. Take care of yourself first, so you can be the source of support and encouragement for others.

CHAPTER NINE

YOUR MISSION STATEMENT

Mission Statement Worksheet

Use the following prompts to help you craft your personal mission statement. Reflect on each question and write down your thoughts.

1. Reflect on Your Core Values

- What principles guide my decisions?

_____

- What do I stand for, even when life gets hard?

_____

- What kind of legacy do I want to leave?

_____

Examples: compassion, resilience, honesty, growth, faith, service

2. Honor Your Healing Journey

- What pain have I transformed into strength?

_____

- What lessons have I learned from grief?

_____

- How do I want to use my healing to help others?

_____

This step is about recasting pain into purpose. Think of how your journey can inspire others.

3. Envision Your Future Intentions

- What kind of person do I want to become?

_____

- What impact do I want to make in my family, community, or profession?

_____

- What dreams am I ready to pursue?

_____

Let your intentions be bold, even if they feel tender.

4. Write It Out

Using the following structure, draft your mission statement:

"My mission is to [action] by [value or principle], so that I can [impact or goal]."

Your Draft:

_____

_____

_____

Tips for Making It Stick

- Keep it visible: Post it somewhere you can see daily (mirror, journal, phone).

- Speak it aloud: Use it as a daily affirmation to reinforce your commitment.

- Revisit and revise: Allow your mission to evolve as you grow and your journey unfolds.

Fill-in-the-Blank Mission Statement

Use this structure to create a succinct mission statement if you prefer a simpler format.

I am committed to _____ (belief, value, or purpose) because I believe _____ (core motivation or reason). My mission is to _____ (action or goal) by _____ (method, approach, or mindset). I will serve _____ (who you want to impact) and stay true to _____ (core values).

Your Fill-in-the-Blank Mission Statement:

_____

_____

_____

Example Mission Statement

I am committed to living with authenticity and compassion **because I believe** that true fulfillment comes from meaningful connection and growth. **My mission is to** empower others to heal and thrive **by** sharing my story, offering support, and leading with empathy. **I will serve** those who feel lost, broken, or uncertain, **and stay true to** my values of honesty, resilience, and kindness. **I will accomplish this by** continuing to learn, reflect, and take intentional action. **The mission** demonstrates **my desire to** leave a legacy of hope and transformation.

If you require further assistance or an accountability partner, please email me at support@wondraspencer.com. I can arrange a one-to-one session with you!

Write a mission statement for personal and professional goals because you will accomplish them!

I **am committed to living** purposefully**, growing with intention, and leading with integrity.** I will strive for excellence in my career by embracing challenges, fostering innovation, and cultivating meaningful relationships. I will nurture my personal growth through self-awareness, resilience, and compassion, celebrating progress over perfection.

I will accomplish my goals because I believe in my vision, trust my journey, and refuse to settle for anything less than the life I can create. Every step I take is a step toward making an impact, achieving fulfillment, and leaving a lasting legacy.

You are claiming your independence and have the motivation and support within you!

Once you've completed this worksheet, please take a moment to reflect on how it reflects your journey and aspirations. Your mission statement is a powerful guiding tool in your life!

CHAPTER TEN

THE POWER WITHIN!

Change and Growth Worksheet

Instructions: Use this workbook to reflect on your personal journey through change. Answer the questions thoughtfully and use the space provided for notes and ideas.

1. Embrace Change with Positivity

- Reflect on a recent change in your life. What emotions did you experience?

- How can you celebrate the excitement and potential that come with this change?

Your thoughts:

_____

_____

_____

2. Set Intentions and Build a Support System

- What are your goals for this new chapter?

- List at least three people who can support you during this transition. How can they help?

Your goals:

_____

_____

_____

Support system:

_____

_____

_____

3. Practice Self-Compassion and Celebrate Achievements

- Identify some emotions you might be feeling during this transition. How can you be gentle with yourself?

- List three accomplishments (big or small) that you want to celebrate.

Your emotions:

_____

_____

_____

Achievements to celebrate:

_____

_____

_____

Tips for Navigating Change

Stay Open-Minded

- What are you curious about in this new phase? Write down any skills or experiences you hope to gain.

Your curiosities:

_____

_____

_____

Set Goals

- What specific goals do you want to achieve? Outline your intentions clearly.

Your intentions:

_____

_____

_____

Build a Support System

- Describe how each support person can help you.

Support person 1:_____

Support person 2:_____

Support person 3:_____

Practice Self-Compassion

- Write a positive affirmation to remind yourself to be kind and gentle during this time.

Your affirmation:

_____

_____

_____

Celebrate Every Success

- How will you celebrate your achievements, no matter how small? Plan at least one thing.

Your celebration plan:

_____

_____

_____

Final Reflection

- Look back at your responses. How does acknowledging your emotions, setting goals, and celebrating successes make you feel about this new chapter?

Your reflection:

_____

_____

_____

Remember, each step forward is an important part of your journey. Rejoice and embrace the possibilities ahead!

CHAPTER ELEVEN
WONDRA'S STORY

Wondra's Story Worksheet

Key Messages

1. Embrace Both Joy and Grief

- Reflect on a personal experience where you felt both joy and sorrow. What did you learn from that experience?

2. Faith as a Guiding Light

- How has your faith (in any form) helped you during difficult times? Share a specific example.

3. The Importance of Self-Care

- List three self-care activities that you enjoy. How do they help you in times of stress or sorrow?

Personal Reflection

1. Think about Wondra's journey:

- What aspects of her story resonate with you?

- How can embracing both joy and grief aid your personal growth?

2. Faith and Trust:

- Identify a moment in your life when faith guided you through a challenging situation.

- Write a short paragraph reflecting on how faith was your compass during that time.

3. Self-Care Practices:

- Describe a time when prioritizing self-care made a difference in your emotional or mental state.

- What plans can you make to incorporate more self-care into your routine?

Important Themes

- Lesson Learned: "Embrace the Hard and Good Days."

- In your own words, explain what this lesson means to you.

- Facing Challenges:

- Write about a "hard day" you experienced. How did it test your resilience?

- What steps did you take to navigate through it?

Celebration of Life

Kaylee's Day:

- Why do you think Wondra chose to celebrate Kaylee's Day with her family?

- How can you honor the memories of loved ones who are no longer with you?

Goals for Growth

1. Short-Term Goals:

- Identify one small goal you can commit to in the next month that aligns with self-care or personal growth.

2. Long-Term Vision:

- What is one long-term goal you have for your personal development? How will you work towards achieving it?

Closing Thoughts

- Write a brief summary of what you learned from Wondra's story and how it inspires you in your own life journey.

Feel free to add more sections or adjust it as needed to fit your needs!

CHAPTER TWELVE

REBUILDING YOUR FUTURE

Chapter Companion: Future Vision Worksheet

Rebuilding Your Life with Purpose and Clarity

This workbook is your blueprint for transformation. Take your time with each section. There are no wrong answers—only honest reflections and bold intentions.

1. Your Vision Statement

Describe the life you want to create. Think about your ideal day, relationships, work, and emotional state.

Prompt: "What does a fulfilling life look like to me?"

Write your vision below:

_____

_____

_____

2. Core Values

List the values guiding your decisions and aligning you with your purpose.

Examples: Faith, Courage, Creativity, Connection, Resilience

My values:

_____

_____

_____

3. Long-Term Goals (1–5 Years)

What dreams are calling you? Be bold. Be specific.

Prompt: "What do I want to accomplish or experience in the next few years?"

My goals:

_____

_____

_____

4. Short-Term Actions (Next 3–6 Months)

Small steps lead to significant change. What can you do now to move toward your vision?

Prompt: "What actions will help me build momentum?"

My action steps:

_____

_____

_____

5. Affirmations for the Journey

Affirmations are powerful reminders of your strength and worth. Write a few that speak to your heart.

Examples: "I am rebuilding with grace." "I am enough." "My future is bright."

My affirmations:

_____

_____

_____

6. Letter to Your Future Self

Write a heartfelt letter to yourself one year from now. Celebrate your growth, encourage your journey, and speak with love.

Dear Future Me,

CHAPTER THIRTEEN

SHARE YOUR STORY

Worksheet: Embracing Healing and Resilience

Chapter Reflection Questions

1. Understanding Resilience

- Reflect on a personal struggle you have faced. How did it contribute to your personal growth?

- What vulnerabilities have you recognized in yourself through this experience?

2. The Power of Connection

- Write about a time when you reached out for support. How did it impact your healing process?

_____

_____

_____

- List three ways you can build or strengthen connections with others who share similar experiences.

_____

_____

_____

3. Transforming Pain into Purpose

- How have your hardships influenced your perspective on life?

- Identify a specific experience that you can use to help others. How might you share this story?

Personal Journey: The Fall

1. Describing Your Fall

- Describe a time when you felt overwhelmed. What led to that moment?

- In your darkest times, what thoughts or feelings did you experience?

2. Finding Strength

- What lessons did you learn during this period of struggle?

- How did you begin to embrace small victories on your journey to recovery?

Turning Point

1. Identifying Your Turning Point

- Write about a moment that changed your perspective on your situation. What was said or done that made a difference?

- What were the initial steps you took towards healing after this moment?

2. Therapeutic Journey

- Describe your experience with therapy or support groups. What emotions did you face, and how did you navigate them?

- What small changes did you implement in your daily life that contributed to your mental well-being?

Transforming Grief into Purpose

1. Finding Purpose in Your Story

- Consider how your pain has shaped who you are today. What have you learned about yourself?

- Write down any creative expressions you've pursued (e.g., writing, art) that channel your experiences into something meaningful.

2. Helping Others

- Reflect on how you can use your understanding of resilience to assist others. What actions can you take?

- What do you hope to accomplish through sharing your story or helping others?

Daily Affirmations

- Create three positive affirmations to remind yourself of your resilience and the journey you are on.

1. _____

2. _____

3. _____

Future Goals

1. Setting Intentions

- What are three goals you want to achieve in your healing journey over the next year?

1. _____

2. _____

3. _____

2. Sustaining Growth

- How will you ensure you continue to support your own mental health and well-being in the future?

Closing Reflection

- Take a moment to reflect on your responses. How do they make you feel about your journey? What steps will you take next to continue embracing healing and resilience?

Feel free to customize this workbook as needed!

CHAPTER FOURTEEN

OPEN LETTER

Worksheet: Embracing the Journey of Healing and Strength

Reflecting on Key Messages

1. You Are Not Alone

- List three challenges you are currently facing.

- Write down three ways you can seek support from others (friends, family, professionals).

2. Believe in Your Strength

- Identify three strengths or qualities you possess that help you during tough times.

- Describe a small step you can take this week toward your healing journey.

3. You Are Worthy and Powerful

- Write a short paragraph about your passions. What lights you up?

- Reflect on a time when you made a positive impact on someone else's life. How did it make you feel?

Breathing Exercise

Before you begin your self-reflection, take a moment for this exercise:

- Take three deep breaths:

- Inhale: Count to four, filling your lungs with air.

- Hold: Count to four, feeling the air expand within you.

- Exhale: Count to four, releasing any tension or negativity.

- Repeat: Do this two more times.

Personal Letter to Yourself

Write a letter to yourself incorporating the key messages from Chapter Fourteen. Use this structure:

- Dear [Your Name],

- Acknowledge your current feelings and experiences.

- Remind yourself that you are not alone in your journey.

- Highlight your strengths and encourage your belief in yourself.

- Affirm your worth and the influence of your unique story.

- Closing:

- End with a personal mantra or affirmation you can repeat daily.

Weekly Check-in

At the end of the week, take time to reflect on your journey:

- What progress have you made toward your healing?

- How did you practice the belief in your strength?

- In what ways did you embrace your worth and power

Final Thoughts

Remember, healing is not linear, and it's okay to take your time. Use this workbook as a guide to support your journey of self-discovery and growth. Stay strong and keep believing in your potential!

CHAPTER FIFTEEN

PAUSE AND LISTEN

Chapter Companion: Past Reflection Worksheet

Honoring Your Journey and Learning from Your Story

Before you build your future, take a moment to reflect on your past. This workbook invites you to explore your experiences, acknowledge your growth, and find meaning in the moments that shaped you.

1. Defining Moments

List 3–5 key experiences that have deeply impacted your life—positively or painfully.

Prompt: "What moments changed, challenged, *or taught me something important?"*

My defining moments:

_____

_____

_____

2. What I've Survived

Name the challenges, losses, or heartbreaks you've endured. Honor your strength.

Prompt: "What have I overcome that once felt impossible?"

I've survived:

_____

_____

_____

3. Lessons Learned

Reflect on what those experiences taught you. What wisdom did you gain?

Examples: "I learned to trust myself." "I discovered my resilience." "I found peace in letting go."

My lessons:

_____

_____

_____

4. How I've Grown

Celebrate your progress. What qualities have you developed? What habits have changed?

Prompt: "How am I different now than I was before?"

I've grown in:

_____

_____

_____

5. Words I Needed Then

Write a message to your past self. What would you say to comfort, encourage, or guide yourself?

Dear Past Me,

_____

_____

_____

6. What I'm Letting Go Of

Release what no longer serves you—guilt, fear, shame, or limiting beliefs.

Prompt: "What am I ready to leave behind?"

I'm letting go of:

_____

_____

_____

CONCLUSION

In conclusion, the reflections and insights gained from this workbook have deepened my understanding of the themes explored in the book. By examining my past experiences and how they relate to the concepts discussed, I've been able to draw meaningful connections that enhance my personal growth. The process has not only highlighted my strengths and areas for improvement but has also instilled a sense of purpose in my journey forward. As I continue to reflect, I hope to apply these lessons in practical ways, ensuring that my past positively informs my future.